The steel tongue drum (aka tong drum, tank dru... pan (aka hank drum, UFO drum, zen drum) are ... help you focus on your feelings, sensations a... training or knowledge of music theory to play them. The main purpose is relaxation, meditation and traveling through your inner world.

No previous training or skills are necessary to enjoy these fascinating instruments. It is impossible to play them incorrectly. Anyone can play them: those who want to develop a good sense of rhythm and an ear for music, those who are seeking relaxation after a hard day at work, those who have always had an interest in learning how to play a musical instrument, and those who want to introduce something unusual into their lives and explore their inner selves.

Both instruments have a unique deep and long sound, and both will sound equally good whether under the experienced musician's hands or a beginner's. Playing the handpan/tongue drum is an intuitive experience which transcends gender, age, culture, and language. It is used by hobbyists, performers, music therapists, cancer patients, educators, and students. You can play it too!

The Handpan

The handpan was designed in Berne, Switzerland by Felix Rohner and Sabina Schärer of PANArt in 2000. The original handpan is famous for its beautiful and deep sound, and although the original instrument is no longer produced, demand for it continues to grow. For this reason, the original PANArt handpan is a collector's item, and often difficult to find.

The handpan is a steel instrument which is played while resting on the musician,s lap. It is constructed from two joined and shaped solid steel sheets, sealed around the edges to create a hollow cavity inside, and hammered to create perfect tonal fields. It can produce seven to nine specific tones, but unlike the steel drums that are synonymous with Carribean music, the handpan goes through a special process called gas-nitriding which hardens the bowls to create an even more exquisite ethereal sound.

The creation of the handpan was based on the design of other instruments such as gongs, gamelan, ghatam, drums, and bells. The width of the metal that forms the instrument is approximately 1mm. The drum vibrates and produces sound depending on the size and shape that is hammered into the steel. Accordingly, the tuning process is a very technical and time consuming process. Normally, there are 9 notes: an eight note scale around the sides and a lower note in the middle. At the bottom of the instrument (known as the "Gu" side), a hole allows the sound to resonate and to be properly amplified thanks to the phenomenon known as Helmholtz Resonance in physics. This resonance that gives the handpan its distinctive sound is the same property that one experiences when blowing across the top of a glass bottle.

The Steel Tongue Drum

The steel tongue drum evolved from the handpan and the wooden tongue drum, which was invented by the Aztecs in Mexico. Other names used for this instrument are the log drum or tone drum. Traditionally the instrument was made from a hollowed log with tuned tongues. The modern version has tongues cut into the top and can be played with mallets, as well as one's hands. The steel tongue drum is a new invention and it is also called the tank drum because some drums were made from a gas tank.

The steel tongue drum gets its unique tone from the vibrations of its tongues of steel. Like the wooden version of this instrument, when the tongue is struck with the finger or a mallet, it vibrates, creating sound waves. The tongues are optimally shaped to achieve the perfect tone and are arranged in such a way that the surrounding notes are musically compatible with each other. By doing this, harmony is created between the notes generated from a particular tongue and the supporting notes of those surrounding it. The multiple harmonic overtones are similar to that of singing bowls or musical bells, and the drum's body creates a resonating chamber that adds depth to the sound.

Main differences between the Steel Tongue Drum and the Handpan

Both the handpan and the steel tongue drum can be played with your hands and used in your lap. While each instrument has its own unique and special sound, there are some differences:

- The steel tongue drum's notes are sustained for longer periods, usually around 8 seconds. The handpan rings for approximately 4 seconds
  The handpan has hammered and distorted strike zones.
  The tongue drum has cut ones.

- A handpan is single-scale tuned and can never be re-tuned. However, while this is true of tongue drums, some new models have multi-scaled tongues that can be re-tuned by adjusting the magnet on the drum.

- The handpan is large (about 24 inches in diameter). The tongue drum is significantly smaller.

- Handpans are more expensive than tongue drums.

- A handpan is very fragile due to its light composite material and the hammered strikes zones. Tongue drums are made of steel.

- The handpan is of African origin, while the tongue drum originated in the Aztec civilization of Mexico.

- The handpan is played by hand, while the steel tongue-drum is sometimes played with mallets, producing a softer sound, almost like raindrops. However, experienced steel tongue drum players can play it using their hands or fingers.

Playing the Steel Tongue Drum

It is important to become acquainted with your steel tongue drum. The sound of the steel tongue drum comes from the vibration of the tongues or slits that are cut out of the top of the instrument.

Tongue drums differ from the handpan in the number of notes and the types of notes which are included on the instrument. Usually, it is a diatonic instrument with one octave plus several notes from other octaves or some chromatic notes. Some may have three C notes and not a single F note. Others have several chromatic notes included.

So while it is based on the regular major diatonic scale, it does not have the typical CDEFGAB arrangement: it can have missing notes, a few additional bass and treble notes placed further away from the main group, or the notes arranged in a variety of ways.

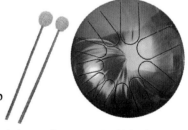

Most steel tongue drums come with mallets. In fact, if you've never played a percussion instrument before, this is the recommended way of playing. With mallets, it is very easy to produce beautiful notes without any effort. Mallets bounce easily on the notes, producing a very clear and deep sound.

Playing with your hands is more enjoyable, but as mentioned, it requires more technical skill and practice. Most popular models of tongue drum have 6 to 15 notes and come in different sizes, from 5.5 to 20 inches. They can be in many tones: major, minor, pentatonic. Some drums have hole octave notes, while some do not. Very often small drums do not include the note F but the note C, D and E exist in two different octaves.

It is important to consider the size of your steel tongue drum. Generally, a smaller drum produces a different sound than that of the larger ones. Most people prefer the sounds produced by larger tongue drums. If you're looking for a more powerful and intense sound, the bigger the instrument, the more volume and reverb it will produce.

Our book is for those who want to try playing simple popular tunes, and not just relax. As mentioned, the keys are tuned in different notes and you need to understand what notes your particular instrument has.

We hope that your tongue drum has at least all the keys for one octave, but because each tongue drum has its particular notes, not all songs from this book will be suitable for you. Just skip them.

To understand what notes your drum has, you need to look at the instructions. Sometimes the notes are indicated by numbers directly on the keys. Stickers with numbers are sometimes included with the drum

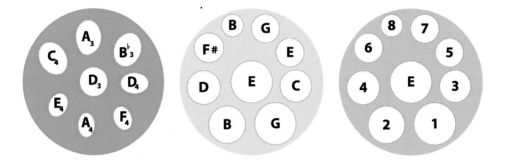

Below is a Short Summary of the Hand Playing Technique:

- Begin to play with mallets, and then you begin to play with your hands. Don't wear rings or any other jewelry while playing.
- Your finger should maintain contact with the surface of the drum for a very short time. The shorter the time of contact with the surface, the longer the sound becomes.
- The quicker your fingers bounce up the drum keys, the richer the overtones will be. Avoid putting your fingers in the middle of the tongue.
- Use the palm to produce force or to extinguish the sound.
- Experiment with different sounds and melodies. No rules - just play whatever you like.

Play by Number

For tongue drums that have numbered musical notation, numbers 1 to 7 represent the keys of the diatonic major scale.

For example, a C Major scale would be:

1 = C (do)
2 = D (re)
3 = E (mi)
4 = F (fa)
5 = G (so / sol)
6 = A (la)
7 = B (ti / si)
8 (1) = C (do)

Dots above or below the numbers indicate a note from a higher or lower octave, respectively.

Your drum can be numbered from 1 to 8, where 8 is note C of the next octave. We use number 1 with a dot above the digit for this note because the most popular models of tongue drums use this numeration.

Most tongue drums include and are tuned to involve the notes of the one octave, and all songs in this book have been simplified for tongue drums and for the beginner without any previous musical experience.

We add a QR code to all songs. Follow the link and listen to the rhythm before beginning to play.

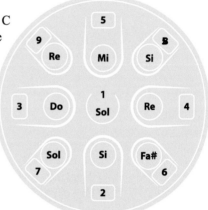

Healing Mantras

Mantras use the energy of sacred sound to bring benefit to the human psyche. This is done through vibration, content, and repetition, and the purpose is to harmonize the energy of one's heart, mind, and body. The creation of this balance of energy has been used for centuries to access and open the human heart and mind and connect them to spiritual powers. Most mantras consist of simple words or sounds that evoke a deep resonance.

Here you will find mantras, mostly in Sanskrit, from different traditions: Hindu, Buddhist, or Sikh. Our easy-to-play sheet music with audio track links will support you in your musical experience, whether it be music playing, individual yoga, or meditation. We are certain that this practice will help you to work through your negative emotions. It's a great natural method of stress relief.

Another one of our books, of Native American songs, also includes shamanic mantras, which are sung with the same goal and used in various healing practices and ceremonies. Chanting a mantra has the ability to affect your state of mind, raise your consciousness, and bring you peace.

Contents

Adi Mantra of Kundalini Yoga*

Ong Na - mo Gu ru - de - v Na - mo---

* Sikh Tradition.

Ayodhya Vasi Ram

Devi Devi Devi Jagan Mohini

Gauri Gauri Gange Rajeshwari

Gayatri Mantra

Govinda Jaya Jaya

Guru Brahma

Hara Hara Mahadeva

Hare Krishna

Hari Hari Bol

Jai Radha Madhav Kunjabihari

Jaya Durge Kali

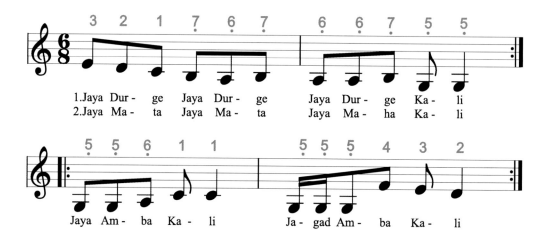

Jaya Ho Mata

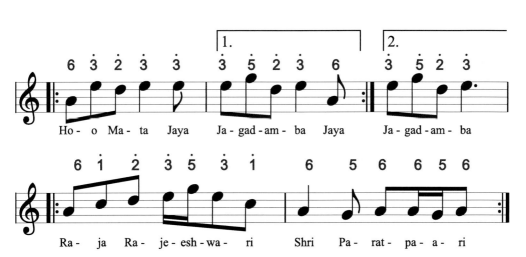

Jyota Se Jyota

** For this mantra, you will need the C#. If you
don't have C#, you can use an ordinary C instead.*

Kali Durgai Namo Namah

Lokah Samastah Sukhino Bhavantu

Maha Mrityunjaya Mantra

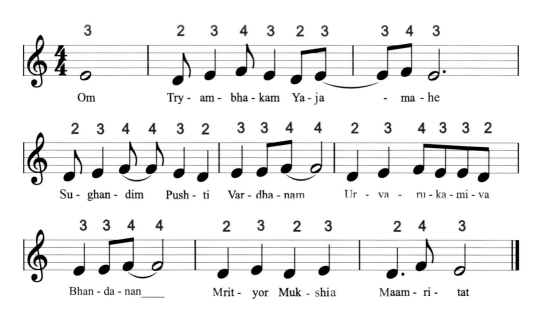

Namosthute

Om Aim Hrim Klim Chamundaye Viche Namaha

Rubato

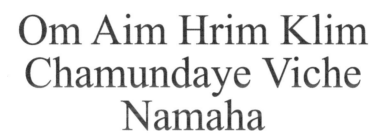

Om Aim Hrim Klim   Cha - mun - da - ye Vi - che

Om Bhagavan

Om Mani Padme Hum

Om Namo Bhagavate Sivanandaya

Om Shakti Om

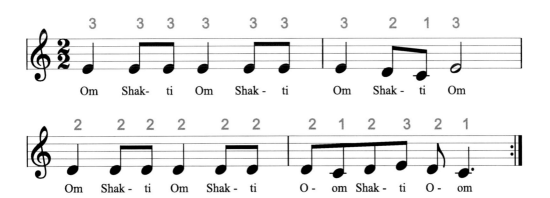

Om Shri Durgayai Namaha

Rama Bolo

Shankara Karunakara

Shiva Shiva Mahadeva

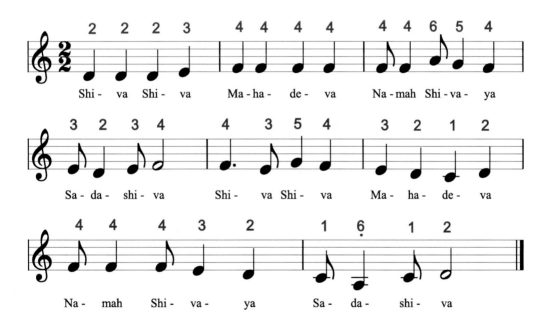

Shiva Shiva Shambho

Shivananda Namah Om

Shivaya Parameshwaraya

Siri Gayatry Mantra*
(Ra Ma Da Sa)

* Sikh Tradition.

Made in the USA
Las Vegas, NV
03 April 2024

88133810R00024